BARBECUE COOKBOOK FOR BEGINNERS

Easy to follow step-by-step guide to grilling and smoking delicious meats 50 recipes

James Walker

All rights reserved.

Disclaimer

The information contained i is meant to serve as a comprehensive collection of strategies that the author of this eBook has done research about. Summaries, strategies, tips and tricks are only recommendation by the author, and reading this eBook will not guarantee that one's results will exactly mirror the author's results. The author of the eBook has made all reasonable effort to provide current and accurate information for the readers of the eBook. The author and it's associates will not be held liable for any unintentional error or omissions that may be found. The material in the eBook may include information by third parties. Third party materials comprise of opinions expressed by their owners. As such, the author of the eBook does not assume responsibility or liability for any third party material or opinions. Whether because of the progression of the internet, or the unforeseen changes in company policy and editorial submission guidelines, what is stated as fact at the time of this writing may become outdated or inapplicable

Table of Contents

INTRODUCTION 8

CHAPTER ONE 16

Grill and Smoked Recipes 16

1. Grilled Pork Steaks 16

2. Grilled Pork Steaks 18

3. Pork Grilled Steaks 20

4. Grilled Pork Ribs 22

5. Pork with Pepper, Ginger and Soy Sauce 25

6. Pork Ribs with Barbecue Sauce ... 27

7. Pork Fillet, Pineapple and Bell Pepper Shashlik 29

8. Grilled Pork Ribs 32

9. Pork Tenderloin Marinated with Mustard Honey 34

10. Grilled Pork Fillet with Avocado Salad 36

11. Pork in Teriyaki Sauce with Vegetable Salad 39

12. Grilled Pork with Mango Salad ... 41

CHAPTER TWO 44

Beef Recipes and Seafoods 44

13. Grilled Beef Tacos with Sweet Potatoes 44

14. Boar Shoulder on The Smoker .. 48

15. Jerky Beef Recipe - Sweet And Spicy 51

16 Mussels with Green Onions And Ginger 54

17 Grilled Shrimps In Aromatic Marinade 56

18 Grilled Seafood Salad and Salsa

Verde With Thai Basil 58

19 Grilled Shrimp with Mint Sauce .. 61

20 Grilled Sea Bass with Vegetables 63

CHAPTER THREE 65

Vegetables Recipes 65

21 Grilled Asparagus 65

22 Grilled Stuffed Bell Pepper 67

23 Zucchini Cutlets 70

24 Orzo Pasta with Grilled Shrimps and Vegetables 72

25 Fried Eggplant with Tomato Sauce 75

26 Grilled Vegetables with Herbs 77

27 Grilled Potatoes and Tomatoes .. 80

28 Sweet Potato Salad...................... 82

CHAPTER FOUR 85

Poultry Recipes 85

29 Chicken Breast Grill with Soya

Sauce 85

30 Chicken Recipe with Sauce 87

31 Savory Chicken Thighs with Grill Marinade 90

32 Organic Grilled Italian Chicken Recipe 92

33 California Grilled Chicken 94

34 Grilled Chicken 96

35 Wings Recipe with Sauce 99

36 Chicken with BBQ Sauce 102

37 Grilled Chicken with Ranch Sauce 104

CHAPTER FIVE 107

Lamb Recipes 107

38 Lamb Shashlik with Honey Sauce 107

39 Grilled Lamb 109

40 Grilled Leg of Lamb 111

41 Lamb (Lamb) Marinated In Anchovy Sauce 113

42 Grilled Leg of Lamb 115

43 Lamb Chops in Lemon-Garlic Marinade 118

44 Grilled Lamb 120

45 Lamb Cutlet Burgers 122

46 Lamb with Mint and Bell Pepper 125

47 Lamb with Yoghurt Sauce 127

48 Lamb Cutlets with Eggplant 129

49 Grilled Lamb with Rhubarb Sauce 131

50 Grilled Lamb with Parsley and Rosemary 134

CONCLUSION 137

INTRODUCTION

if you enjoy a good barbecue every once in a while, you're missing out if you aren't with Traeger After all, Traeger's are wood-fired grills. At the end of the day, wood and propane always win. The taste of cooking your meat on a wood- or charcoal fire gives you is superior to anything else. Cooking your meat on wood imparts an excellent flavour.

With any other pellet grill, you'll have to constantly monitor the fire to avoid flare-ups, making it a pain in the ass to baby sit However, Traeger has built-in technology to ensure that pellets are fed regularly. To see how hot the grill is it measures and adds or removes wood to/pellets to control the temperature Naturally, a Traeger grill has a simple to use temperature control knob

You can choose from cheap grills to expensive grills by Traeger. Choose one between 19,500

BTU or 36,000 BTU. Anything is also possible. Grill performance varies with grilling intensity. They are not just grills. They are also mixers. The whole cooking area is obscured by hoods that you can pull down. Heat is forced into the cooking area It is likely that hot air and smoke will be evenly distributed while your food cooks in the pot because of this.

Additionally, a Traeger grills are also a convection oven. Generally speaking, Traeger's are pretty forgiving. Just to illustrate... you can use a Traeger to cook a steak, as well as well as a pizza. Even more.

It uses less power as well. Initial set-up takes 300 watts. but only the start of the process. After that, the light bulb uses only 50 watts of power.

What is the Barbecue? Smoking or Grilling?

Yes, and no. Although the most common usage of the term "barbecue" describes the backyard grill, some people have a different definition of the term. Barbecue can be divided into two categories: hot and fast and low and slow.

Grilling generally uses a direct heat that ranges between 300-500 degrees. It does a great job on steak, chicken, chops, and fish. While the food will cook, you must watch it closely to avoid burning. It will pick up less smoky flavor. Mostly, this is a simple and enjoyable way to cook; you have plenty of time to hang out with your friends and family during the cookout. It is low and slow. Indirect heat and temperatures in a smoker typically run between 200-275. If you've ever been to Kansas City, Memphis, or Texas, you know what I'm talking about. A slow- and low-smoked piece of meat can take anywhere from 2 to 15 hours to fully develop its natural flavour. When you look into a slow smoked meat, pink "smoke ring" means the meat has been in the smoker for a long time

How to Use Wood in BBQ Smokers

The essence of good barbecue smoking is wood. It's what gives the dish its flavour. Wood was once the only fuel available, but controlling the temperature and amount of smoke reaching the meat is difficult. The majority of people nowadays use charcoal, gas, pellet, or electric smokers. The wood is added in chunks, pellets, or sawdust, and it smoulders and produces a nice amount of smoke.

The most common beginner mistake is oversmoking the meat. Beginners should begin with a small amount of wood and work their way up. It's a common misconception that you should soak the wood before installing it, but it doesn't make much of a difference. Wood does not absorb water well and evaporates quickly. When you put soaked wood on charcoal coals, it cools them down, and you want to keep the temperature consistent when smoking meats.

Depending on the type of wood you use, the flavour you get varies. The best kind of wood is dry, non-green wood. It's important to avoid sap-containing woods like pines, cedar, fir, Cyprus, spruce, or redwood when choosing wood. The sap imparts an off-putting flavour to the meat. Also, scraps of lumber should never be used because they are usually treated with chemicals. It's not a good idea to smoke a barbecue. Hickory, apple, alder, and mesquite are some of the most popular woods. Hickory and mesquite give meat a powerful flavour, so it's best for heavily spiced meats like ribs. Apple and alder wood produce a sweeter, lighter smoke that is ideal for meats that aren't overly spiced, such as fish and chicken.

You can toss the chips right in with the charcoal in a charcoal BBQ smoker. Wood chunks work best on gas grills. If you're having trouble getting the wood chunks to smoulder, try wrapping them in tin foil and cutting slits in the top. Place the wood chunks in a foil bag on top of the hot coals. In a few minutes, the wood should begin to smoulder. It's critical to incorporate the wood into the barbecue smoking process as soon as possible. Smoke is absorbed more readily by cold meat.

You should always weigh the amount of wood you put in. This allows you to fine-tune the amount each time to achieve the desired effect. Depending on the thickness of the meat, the amount will vary. For ribs, 8 ounces for brisket and pulled pork, and 2 ounces for chicken, turkey, and fish, use about 4 ounces of wood. If the wood starts to burn or there is a long barbecue smoke, you may need to get creative. To insulate the wood further, place it in an iron skillet on top of the coals. For longer barbecue smokes, you can also make a so-called smoke bomb. Fill one foil pan with enough water to cover the wood chips, and the other with enough water to cover the wood chips. The one that isn't wet will start to smoulder right away.

When the water from the second one evaporates, it will ignite and smoulder. You won't have to keep opening the door to add more wood this way.

CHAPTER ONE
Grill and Smoked Recipes

1. Grilled Pork Steaks

INGREDIENTS

- Ten pork steaks 2 cm thick
- Coarsely ground red chili
- Black polka dots
- 4-5 tbsp. olive oil ☐ 2.5-3 tbsp. honey
- 5 h l Dijon mustard
- 4 cloves garlic
- Salt
- 1 tbsp. lemon juice
- 2 pinches dry oregano

PREPARATION

1. Grind black peas in a mortar. We washed the meat, make small cuts on the sides of the meat so that it does not bend, and dipped it with a paper towel. Salt, sprinkle with chili, then ground black pepper on both sides.
2. Making the sauce. We mix honey, mustard, lemon juice. Press the garlic through a press, add to the sauce. Stir, pour in the oil. Mix again. Put the meat in a bowl, pour over the sauce, and sprinkle with oregano. We mix. Cover with foil, leave to marinate for an hour at room temperature and stir once a hour.
3. We heat the pan. Reduce heat to medium and lay out the meat. Fry for 4-5 minutes on each side. Enjoy your meal!

2. Grilled Pork Steaks

INGREDIENTS

- 3 servings
- 500 grams pork
- Salt
- Black peppercorns
- Rosemary
- 1 a tomato
- 1 clove garlic large
- Vegetable oil for lubrication

PREPARATION

1. Cut the steaks from a piece of meat. Season them with salt, pepper and grease with vegetable oil. Preheat the grill pan.

Lay out the steaks and fry each for 3 minutes on each side, changing the pattern. At the end of frying, sprinkle the steaks with rosemary, add tomato and garlic.

2. Put the pan in the oven and on the grill mode hold it there for a few minutes to completely fry the meat.

3. Pork Grilled Steaks

INGREDIENTS

- 6 steaks shoulder blades (pork)
- 3 heads Luke
- 1 tsp Salt
- 05 tsp Ground black pepper
- 0.5 tsp Ground paprika

PREPARATION

1. we beat the pork
2. Add salt, black pepper, paprika, onion - mix ... Remove for 2 hours in a warm place ...
3. Put on the wire rack and fry on each side for 15 minutes ... 30 minutes in total ...
4. The steaks are ready, bon appetite

4. Grilled Pork Ribs

INGREDIENTS

- Pork ribs - 2 pcs. (4 kg) ☐ White sugar - 1 tbsp.
- Chili powder - 1 tbsp.
- Ground cumin - 1/2 tsp.
- Salt to taste
- Ground black pepper - to taste For glaze:
- Maple syrup - 3/4 cup

- Chili pepper (seeded and finely chopped) - 1 pc.
- Hot sauce - 3 tbsp.
- Ketchup - 2 tbsp.
- Dijon mustard - 1.5 tbsp.
- Apple cider vinegar - 1 tbsp.

PREPARATION

1. Grease the grill grate with vegetable oil and turn on the grill for preheating to 150-180 degrees.
2. In a small bowl, combine the sugar, chilli, cumin, 4 teaspoons of salt and 1 teaspoon of black pepper. Grate ribs with this spicy mixture and set aside.
3. When the grill has warmed up enough, put the ribs on the grill with bacon, cover, grill the pork ribs until tender, about 1.5 hours.
4. Meanwhile, prepare the icing. In a medium bowl, combine maple syrup,

chili, hot sauce, ketchup, mustard and vinegar. Continuing to grill the pork ribs with the lid closed, brush them with this glaze every 2-3 minutes, until a caramel crust forms (this will take about 15 minutes). Transfer the finished ribs to a dish, grease with the remaining icing, allow to soak and serve immediately.

5. Pork with Pepper, Ginger and Soy Sauce

INGREDIENTS

- Pork meat (tenderloin) - 450 g ☐ Chili pepper, seeded - 1 pc.
- Garlic - 3 cloves
- Fresh ginger - 1 piece (5 cm) ☐ Green onions - 5 pcs.
- Olive oil - 2 tbsp.
- Soy sauce - 4 tbsp.
- Rice vinegar (or other soft vinegar) - 4 tbsp
- Honey - 1 tbsp.
- Salt
- Ground black pepper

PREPARATION

1. Preheat your barbecue or grill (charcoal).
2. Finely chop the chili pepper, garlic, ginger and green onion. On a piece of meat, make diagonal cuts (up to half) at a distance of 3 cm from each other. Stir all ingredients except pork. Season with salt and pepper to taste. Brush the cooked mixture over the pork so that it falls into the cuts in the meat.
3. Barbecue the meat for about 20 minutes, turning frequently (gently). Transfer to a serving dish and leave in a warm place for 10 minutes.
4. Slice the meat diagonally (opposite) into 1 cm slices. Serve with the cabbage salad. Enjoy your meal!

6. Pork Ribs with Barbecue Sauce

INGREDIENTS

- Salt - 1 tbsp
- Ground black pepper - 1 tbsp ☐ Ground red pepper - 1/2 tsp. ☐ Pork ribs - 3 strips (about 2.5 kg) ☐ Lime (cut into halves) - 2 pcs.
- Barbecue sauce

PREPARATION

1. Remove the film from the ribs. In a small bowl, combine salt, red and black peppers.
2. Grate the pork ribs on all sides with a slice of lime. Then sprinkle with a mixture of salt and pepper on all sides.

Wrap the ribs in plastic wrap, put them in a baking sheet and refrigerate for 8 hours so that they are fully saturated with pepper and salt (marinated).

3. Switch on the oven with grill function to preheat to 180 degrees. Remove the ribs from the refrigerator, remove the foil and place on the wire rack. Grill the pork ribs in the oven until brown, for about 40 minutes. Then brush the ribs with barbecue sauce and bake for another 30 minutes.
4. Serve hot fried pork ribs, drizzle with remaining barbecue sauce.

7. Pork Fillet, Pineapple and Bell Pepper Shashlik

INGREDIENTS

- Pineapple, canned in pieces - 230 g ☐ Apple cider vinegar - 2 tbsp. l + 1 1/2 tsp ☐ Brown sugar - 2 tbsp l.
- A pinch of ground black pepper
- Pork fillet (cut into 2.5 cm pieces) - 250 g
- Bulgarian red pepper (cut into cubes 1.3 cm) - 1/2 pc.
- Bulgarian green pepper (cut into cubes 1.3 cm) - 1/2 pc.
- Cooked rice for garnish (optional)

PREPARATION

1. Drain the pineapple, reserve the juice. Put the pineapple in a bowl and refrigerate. In a bowl, combine pineapple juice, vinegar, brown sugar and black pepper. Pour half of the marinade into a large plastic bag with fasteners, and put the chopped pork fillet there. Fasten the bag, shake well and put in the refrigerator for 4 hours. Cover the rest of the marinade and refrigerate.
2. Turn on the grill to preheat to medium temperature. Remove the meat from the marinade. On metal or wooden (soaked in water) skewers, string meat, pineapple and pepper in turn. Place the pork kebabs with pineapple and pepper on the grill and cook, covered, for about 10-15 minutes, brushing with the reserved marinade and turning.

3. Serve pork kebabs with pineapple and pepper with boiled rice (optional)

8. Grilled Pork Ribs

INGREDIENTS

- Pork ribs - 2.7 kg
- Peach nectar - 3 cups
- Unsalted tomato sauce - 420 g
- Onions (finely chopped) - 1 glass
- Brown sugar - 1/2 cup
- Salt - 1 tsp
- Mustard powder - 1 tbsp
- A mixture of five spices - 2 tsp
- Garlic powder - 1 tsp
- Ground black pepper - 1 tsp.
- Soy sauce - 1/3 cup
- Rice vinegar - 1/4 cup
- Spicy sauce (hot) - 2-3 tsp.

PREPARATION

1. In a small bowl, combine brown sugar, salt, mustard powder, five spice mixture, garlic powder and black pepper. Remove fat from the ribs. Grate the ribs on all sides with a spicy mixture and put them

on a baking sheet, cover and refrigerate overnight.
2. Place a container under the grill to drain the juice. Put the ribs on a wire rack, meat up and fry under a closed lid for 1.5-1.75 hours.
3. Meanwhile, prepare the sauce. In a large saucepan, combine the nectar, tomato sauce, onions, soy sauce, vinegar and hot sauce. Bring the sauce to a boil over medium heat, reduce the heat and simmer the sauce, uncovered, for about 50 minutes, until thickened (you should make about 3 glasses of sauce). Brush the ribs with sauce every 15 minutes.
4. Serve the ribs with the remaining sauce.

9. Pork Tenderloin Marinated with Mustard Honey

INGREDIENTS

- Pork tenderloin - 900 g
- Honey - 2/3 cup
- Dijon mustard - 0.5 cups
- Ground chili pepper - 0.25-0.5 tsp
- Salt - 0.25 tsp

PREPARATION

1. Place the pieces of pork tenderloin in a tight bag (or a suitable container with a lid). Separately mix the remaining ingredients for the honey mustard marinade with the hot pepper.

2. Set aside 2/3 cup of the marinade. Pour the remaining marinade over the meat. Turn the meat over in the bag so that it is completely marinated. Put honey marinated pork in refrigerator for at least 4 hours. Turn over from time to time.
3. Drain the marinade. Cook pork in a closed grill over medium heat for 8-9 minutes on each side (for finished meat, the juice released when piercing should be transparent).
4. Heat the remaining mustard-honey marinade sauce in a gravy boat. Drizzle over the meat when serving.

10. Grilled Pork Fillet with Avocado Salad

- Pork fillet (cut into slices 2 cm thick) - 2 pcs. (400 g each)
- Red onion (finely chopped) - 1/2 cup
- Lime juice - 1/2 cup
- Chili (seeded and finely chopped) - 1/4 cup
- Olive oil - 2 tbsp. Ground cumin (cumin) - 4 tsp.

For the salad:

- Medium avocado (diced) - 2 pcs.
- Cream tomatoes (diced) - 2 pcs.
- Small cucumber (peeled and diced) - 1 pc.
- Green onions (chopped) - 2 pcs.

- Fresh cilantro (chopped) - 2 tbsp.
- Liquid honey - 1 tbsp.   Salt - 1/4 tsp.
- Ground black pepper - 1/4 tsp.   Chili jelly - 3 tbsp.
- Vegetable oil for grilling grill

PREPARATION

1. In a small bowl, combine red onions, lime juice, chili peppers, olive oil and cumin. Pour 1/2 cup of the resulting marinade into a large plastic bag with fasteners, and put the chopped pork fillet into it. Fasten the bag and mix its contents well. Put the bag of meat in the refrigerator for 2 hours. Take another 1/3 cup from the remaining marinade, cover and set aside. Pour the remaining marinade into a large bowl, put the avocado, tomatoes, cucumber, green onions, cilantro, honey, salt and black pepper in the same place, stir, cover and refrigerate until serving.

2. In a small saucepan, combine the reserved marinade, 1/3 cup, and the chili jelly. Bring to a boil over medium heat and cook, stirring occasionally, for about 2 minutes.
3. Grease the grill rack with vegetable oil and turn on the grill to preheat to medium temperature. Remove the pork fillet from the bag with the marinade and put on the grill, grill the pork without covering, for about 4-6 minutes on each side, greasing with the contents of the saucepan.
4. Serve pork fillet with avocado and tomato salad.

11. Pork in Teriyaki Sauce with Vegetable Salad

INGREDIENTS

- Pork - 500 g
- Carrots - 200 g (1 pc.)
- Zucchini or zucchini - 200 g (1 pc.)
- Green beans (fresh or frozen) - 150 g
- Teriyaki sauce with honey - 50 ml
- Orange juice - 30 ml
- Olive oil - 30 ml
- Sesame - 15 g

PREPARATION

1. Prepare all the pork ingredients in the teriyaki sauce. Wash, peel and dry the vegetables. Do the same with meat.

2. Grate zucchini or young zucchini on the same grater in a bowl with carrots.
3. Cut the beans in half. Combine vegetables and set aside.
4. Cut the pork into small cubes.
5. String the pieces of meat on wooden skewers, previously soaked in water.
6. Brush the pork with honey teriyaki sauce and place on the grill or barbecue rack.
7. have a grill pan, you can grill or open fire. Grill the meat for about 20 minutes until tender, brushing occasionally with sauce.
8. For dressing, combine sesame seeds, orange juice and vegetable oil. Mix the vegetables in a bowl.
9. Put the salad from zucchini, carrots and beans on a plate, add the sauce to the salad and stir. Place the pork skewer on top.

10. A delicious and nutritious pork dish is ready!

12. Grilled Pork with Mango Salad

INGREDIENTS

- Natural yogurt without additives - 2 tbsp.
- Honey - 2 tsp.   Garlic (chopped) - 2 cloves
- White wine vinegar - 1 tsp ☐ Ground cumin (cumin) - 1/2 tsp.
- Salt - 1/4 tsp.
- Ground turmeric - 1/4 tsp.   Garlic powder - 1/8 tsp

- Ground cinnamon - 1/8 tsp. Ground red pepper - 1/8 tsp.
- A pinch of ground ginger. Whole pork cutlets - 4 pcs. (110 g each)

For the salad:

- Large mango (peeled and diced) - 1 pc.
- Red onion (finely chopped) - 3/4 cup
- Fresh tomatoes (diced) - 3/4 cup
- Fresh chili pepper (seeded and finely chopped) - 1/2 pc.
- Lime juice - 2 tsp
- Salt - 1/4 tsp. Vegetable oil for grilling grill

PREPARATION

1. In a large plastic bag, combine yogurt, honey, garlic, vinegar, cumin, salt, turmeric, garlic powder, cinnamon, red pepper and a pinch of ground ginger. Put pork cutlets into this marinade, close

the bag, shake well and put in the refrigerator for 2 hours.

2. Meanwhile, in a bowl, combine all the ingredients for the salad, stir and leave at room temperature for 1 hour. Then cover and refrigerate.

3. Grease the grill rack with vegetable oil and turn on the grill to preheat to medium temperature. Take the bag of meat out of the refrigerator, remove the pork cutlets from the bag and place on the grill. Grill pork with the lid closed, about 6-10 minutes on each side (the meat thermometer should show a temperature of 80 degrees).

4. Serve pork cutlets with mango salad.

CHAPTER TWO
Beef Recipes and Seafoods

13. Grilled Beef Tacos with Sweet Potatoes

INGREDIENTS

- Beef
- 1 lb (450 g) beef flank, cut into 2 pieces
- 1 onion, quartered
- 30 ml (2 tablespoons) of vegetable oil
- 30 ml (2 tablespoons) brown sugar
- 30 ml (2 tablespoons) lime juice
- 15 mL (1 tablespoon) soy sauce
- 1 ml (1/4 teaspoon) Tabasco Jalapeno Sauce
- 2.5 mL (1/2 teaspoon) Cayenne pepper, Garnish
- 2 sweet potatoes, peeled and cubed

- 30 ml (2 tablespoons) of vegetable oil
- 12 soft corn tortillas about 15 cm (6 inches) in diameter
- 1 avocado, peeled and sliced
- Sour cream, to taste
- Hot chipotle sauce, to taste
- Lime wedges, to taste

PREPARATION

Beef

1. In an airtight bag or in a dish, mix all ingredients. Close the bag or cover the dish. Refrigerate 8 hours or overnight. Drain the meat and onions. Discard the marinade.

2. Place a barbecue wok on the barbecue grill. Preheat the barbecue to high power.

   Oil the grill.

Garnish

3. Overlay two large sheets of aluminum foil. In the center, add the sweet

potatoes. Oil, salt and pepper. Close the wrapper tightly.

4. Place the foil on the grill, close the lid and cook for 20 minutes, turning the foil halfway through cooking. Remove the sweet potatoes and crush them roughly with a fork. Keep the mashed pot warm.

5. In the meantime, cook the onion in the barbecue wok until it begins to brown. Grill the meat for 3-5 minutes on each side for rare cooking. Salt and pepper. Let the meat rest on a plate for 5 minutes.

   Reheat the tortillas on the grill.

6. On a work surface, thinly slice the meat. Spread tortillas with sweet potato puree.

   Garnish with sliced beef, onions and avocado. Serve with sour cream, chipotle sauce and lime wedges, if desired.

14. Boar Shoulder on The Smoker

Yield 6-8 servings

INGREDIENTS

- Shoulder of boar 4 lbs (2.2 kg)

- 1/4 cup Worcestershire sauce
- 1/4 cup soy sauce
- 2 cloves garlic, chopped
- 1/2 spoon. dry mustard
- 1/4 cup of olive oil
- 1/2 cup red wine
- juice of 1 lime.   juice of 1 lemon
- 1/2 cup orange juice
- 1/4 spoon. black pepper cracked
- 1 tablespoon chopped rosemary
- 1 tablespoon chopped sage
- 1 tablespoon chopped coriander

PREPARATION

1. In a large bowl, combine all ingredients except wild boar.
2. Cover and let rest 1 to 2 hours to allow the flavors to get married.
3. Place boar shoulder in a large saucepan and garnish with marinade, rubbing well

in the meat. You can also put it in a ziplock bag

4. Cover and refrigerate for 4 to 6 hours. Remove the meat from the marinade, reserving the marinade.
5. Prepare a smoking pit or electric smoker at a temperature of 250 ° to 300 ° F or according to the manufacturer's instructions, using Mesquite and Pecan wood.
6. Boar shoulder smoke for 3 to 4 hours or until the internal temperature reaches 165 ° F, basting with the marinade every 30 minutes. If using a rack, bake at an internal temperature of 135 - 138 ° F for medium-rare or desired cooking. Slice and serve as wild boar.

15. Jerky Beef Recipe - Sweet And Spicy

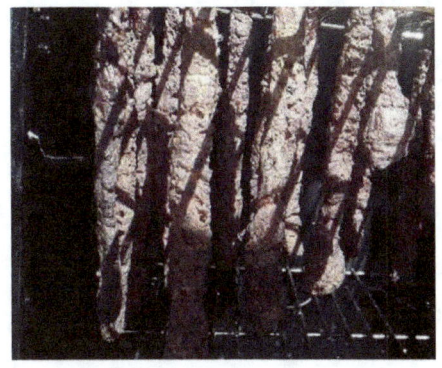

INGREDIENTS

- 1 lb of indoor Round
- Marinade
- 1 C. Redhot Sauce
- 1 C. Ground Ginger
- 1/3 cup of Soy Sauce
- 1/2 cup Teriyaki sauce

- 1/2 cup of Worcestershire sauce
- 1 C. Tabasco
- 1 C. Lemon Juice
- 1 C. tablespoon Garlic Salt
- 1 C. Onion Powder
- 1 C. Ground Pepper
- 1/2 cup of brown sugar

PREPARATION

1. Whisk together all ingredients (except meat) in a large glass bowl.
2. Add the beef strips (deer, moose or other) and mix to immerse completely in the marinade. Cover and marinate in refrigerator for 24 hours. Stir a few times during marinating.
3. Remove the meat from the marinade and discard the remaining marinade. Spread the meat strips on the shelves of the smoker or hang them without

touching them. Take your favorite woods for smoking.

4. Put on the smoker for 6 to 8 hours at low temperature without water tray 160F - 70C. They should remain soft enough to bend without breaking. Keep in an airtight container.

16 Mussels with Green Onions And Ginger

INGREDIENTS

- 2 tables. l. - olive oil
- 1 table. l. - chopped ginger
- 3-4 pcs. - a clove of garlic
- 1 PC. - chili peppers
- 2 bunches - green onions
- ½ glass - dry white wine
- 20 pcs. - peeled mussels
- 4 tables. l. – butter ☐ To taste - salt.

PREPARATION

1. Preheat the grill to a medium temperature of 110 degrees.

2. Pour olive oil into a container, put butter.Once the oil is hot, add chopped garlic, finely chopped hot peppers, ginger root and half a green onion.
3. Cook for no more than 1 minute.
4. Add mussels, pour in wine (can be replaced with water), stir quickly.
5. Cook with the lid closed for 5 minutes (stirring occasionally). The mussels are ready when they open.
6. Salt is added at the end of cooking.
7. Transfer the hot seafood to a dish, sprinkle with the remaining onions on top.

17 Grilled Shrimps In Aromatic Marinade

INGREDIENTS

- 800 g - peeled shrimp
- 1 table. l. - olive oil
- 3 tables. l. - melted butter
- 6 cloves – garlic
- 2 tables. l. – honey
- 2 tables. l. - lime juice
- 1/2 tea l. – salt
- To taste - ground red and black pepper.

PREPARATION

1. Mix butter with olive oil. Add lime juice, honey, and minced garlic.

2. Separately mix salt, black and red pepper. Spicy herbs can be added if desired.
3. Sprinkle the shrimp with the dry mixture, stir. Then let sit for 15 minutes.
4. Pour the cooked marinade over, then string on wooden sticks or skewers.
5. Preheat the grill to 160 degrees. Place the seafood on the wire rack.
6. Cook each side for 3 minutes. The shrimp are fully cooked when they turn transparent.
7. Serve hot to the table.

18 Grilled Seafood Salad and Salsa Verde With Thai Basil

INGREDIENTS

- Salsa verde
- 30 g (1 cup) Thai basil leaves
- 30 g (1 cup) coriander leaves
- 1/4 cup (60 mL) vegetable oil
- 45 ml (3 tablespoons) lime juice
- 30 ml (2 tablespoons) of water
- 1 green onion, cut into sections
- Seafood and vegetables
- 900 g (2 lb) of mussels, cleaned

- 225 g (1/2 lb) medium shrimp (31-40), shelled and deveined
- 4 small squid, trimmed
- 15 ml (1 tablespoon) vegetable oil
- 15 ml (1 tablespoon) lime juice
- 10 ml (2 teaspoons) fish sauce (nuocmam)
- 2 teaspoons (10 mL) turmeric
- 1 bulb of fennel, thinly sliced with mandolin
- 400 g (2 cups) baby potatoes, cooked
- 2 green onions, chopped
- 1 tomato, quartered
- Thai basil leaves, to taste

PREPARATION

1. Salsa verde
2. In the food processor, finely grind all the ingredients.
3. Seafood and vegetables

4. Preheat the barbecue to high power. Oil the grill.
5. In a large bowl, combine mussels, shrimp, squid, oil, lime juice, fish sauce and turmeric. Salt and pepper.
6. Place the mussels directly on the barbecue grill. Close the barbecue lid and cook the mussels for 3 to 5 minutes or until they are all open. Discard those that remain closed. Place in a bowl. Shell the mussels (keep some for service, if desired).
7. Grill shrimp and squid for 2 to 3 minutes per side or until shrimp and squid are cooked and browned. On a work surface, cut squid into 1 cm (1/2 inch) slices.
8. Place the fennel in a bowl. Lightly oil, then season with salt and pepper.

9. Spread seafood and vegetables on plates. Sprinkle salsa verde and garnish with Thai basil leaves.

19 Grilled Shrimp with Mint Sauce

INGREDIENTS

- 500 g shrimp

For Sauce

- Half of fresh mint
- 1 - 2 shallots
- 3 cloves of garlic
- 2 tablespoons apple cider vinegar
- 1 tea glass of olive oil
- 1 teaspoon of sugar
- 2 teaspoons of salt

- 1 teaspoon of red paprika

PREPARATION

1. For the sauce, put all ingredients except olive oil into the blender and run the blender. Slowly add olive oil and have a thick consistency. Extract the shrimps and put them in a deep dish. Hover over the sauce and find all sides. Wrap the stretch film and leave in the refrigerator for at least 2-3 hours. Pass the prawns to the bottle. Cook on overheated grill. Serve hot.

20 Grilled Sea Bass with Vegetables

INGREDIENTS

- 2 perch
- 1 onion
- 2 cloves of garlic
- 1 potato
- 1 carrot
- 1 lemon
- 2 sprigs of rosemary

For Sauce

- 1 tea glass of olive oil
- 2 cloves of crushed garlic
- 1 teaspoon red ground pepper

- 1 teaspoon of red paprika
- 1 teaspoon black pepper
- 2 teaspoons of salt

PREPARATION

1. Clean the perch. Slice all vegetables to be very thin. You filled the fish with vegetables.
2. Add the rosemary. Mix the ingredients for the sauce thoroughly with a fork.
3. Tie the fish with the rope and take them to the barbecue.
4. Brush with the help of the sauce you prepare and cook the fish duplex. Serve.

CHAPTER THREE
Vegetables Recipes

21 Grilled Asparagus

INGREDIENTS

- Water - 1 glass
- Fresh asparagus - 450 g
- BBQ sauce - 1/4 cup

PREPARATION

1. In a large skillet, bring 1 cup water to a boil. Put the asparagus in boiling water, cover the pan with a lid and blanch the asparagus for about 4-6 minutes, until completely soft. Remove the asparagus

from the water and transfer to a paper towel, blot well to remove all liquid.

2. Soak wooden skewers in cold water for 5 minutes so that they do not burn during frying. Turn on the grill to preheat to medium heat.
3. String the cooled asparagus on wooden skewers (as shown in the photo).
4. Place the asparagus on the grill rack and cook, uncovered, for about 1 minute on each side. Then brush the asparagus with barbecue sauce and cook for about 2 minutes more, turn over, grease the other side with the sauce and cook for about 1 minute.
5. Serve the asparagus immediately.

22 Grilled Stuffed Bell Pepper

INGREDIENTS

- Olive oil - 1/2 cup + 2 tsp.
- Parmesan cheese (shredded on a grater) - 3/4 cup
- Fresh basil leaves - 2 cups
- Sunflower seeds (kernels) or walnuts (kernels) - 2 tbsp.
- Garlic - 4 cloves
- Bulgarian pepper (seeded and finely chopped) - 1/2 cup
- Corn grains (canned) - 4 cups
- Medium sized bulgarian pepper - 4 pcs.

- Parmesan cheese (grated) (for serving) - 1/4 cup

PREPARATION

1. Switch on the grill to preheat to medium temperature.
2. Prepare the pesto sauce. Pour 1/2 cup olive oil into the bowl of a food processor or blender, add 3/4 cup cheese, basil, seeds (or nuts) and garlic, pulsate until smooth.
3. In a large skillet, heat the remaining olive oil, add the chopped bell pepper and fry, stirring occasionally, until soft. Add corn and pesto to the pan and stir well.
4. Cut a whole bell pepper into halves, remove seeds and stalks. Place the halves on a preheated grill, slices down. Place the lid on the grill and cook the peppers for about 8 minutes. Then stuff

the pepper halves with the corn mixture and grill for another 4-6 minutes, until the pepper is soft.
5. Serve the finished dish sprinkled with Parmesan.

23 Zucchini Cutlets

INGREDIENTS

- Zucchini - 750 g
- Salt and black pepper
- Egg (slightly beaten) - 1 pc. ☐ Coarse flour - 2/3 cup (60 g) ☐ Chopped nutmeg - 1/4 tsp.

For the sauce:

- Lemon zest - 1 tsp ☐ Lemon juice - 1 tbsp.
- Mint (chopped) - 3-4 tbsp.
- Fat-free yogurt (natural) - 150 g

PREPARATION

1. Grind the zucchini with a blender or on a fine grater, season with salt, leave for 30 minutes at room temperature. Then rinse in a colander under running cold water. Squeeze well with your hands and put on a paper towel, blot.

2. Transfer the chopped zucchini to a bowl and add the egg, flour, nutmeg and pepper. Mix everything well and let it brew at room temperature for 20 minutes.
3. Prepare the sauce. In a separate bowl, combine lemon, zest, mint and yogurt. Cover and refrigerate.
4. Heat a skillet or skillet over medium heat. Spoon the zucchini mixture (1 tablespoon each) into the pan and gently form the patties. Fry for 3-4 minutes on each side.

   Serve with yoghurt sauce.

24 Orzo Pasta with Grilled Shrimps and Vegetables

INGREDIENTS

- Orzo pasta - 230 g
- Zucchini or yellow zucchini (cut into 0.5 cm slices) - 2 pcs. (about 260 g)
- Bulgarian red or yellow pepper (seeded and cut into quarters) - 1 pc.
- Pesto sauce - 3 tbsp., Fresh lime juice - 2 tablespoons
- Fresh or frozen shrimp (uncooked) (peeled) - 450 g
- Fresh tomatoes (peeled and cut into 1 cm cubes) - 250 g

- Extra virgin olive oil - 6.5 tbsp., Red wine vinegar - 4 tbsp.
- Fresh basil leaves (cut into strips) - ½ cup
- Mozzarella cheese (cut into 1 cm cubes) - 230 g
- Fresh basil leaves for serving

PREPARATION

1. Prepare the ortso pasta in salted water, according to the instructions on the package. Dry the paste, rinse under running cold water, dry again. Transfer to a large bowl and mix with 1 tablespoon of olive oil.
2. Turn on the grill to preheat to medium temperature. In a small bowl, combine 2 tablespoons of oil and 2 tablespoons of vinegar. Grease the zucchini and pepper with an oil mixture, sprinkle with salt and pepper. Mix pesto, lime juice, 3.5

tablespoons oil, and 2 tablespoons vinegar separately. Place the shrimps in a medium bowl and drizzle with 2 tablespoons of pesto vinegar, stir.

3. Place the zucchini and peppers on the grill rack and fry until crispy, about 3-4 minutes on each side. Transfer vegetables to a cutting board. Sprinkle the shrimps with salt and pepper, place on the grill and cook for about 2-3 minutes on each side. Put the fried shrimp in a bowl with ortso. Cut the zucchini and bell pepper into cubes and place in a bowl with ortso. Add remaining pesto vinegar, tomatoes, chopped basil and cheese. Season with salt and pepper to taste, mix well.

4. Serve the dish sprinkled with basil leaves immediately or chill in the refrigerator.

25 Fried Eggplant with Tomato Sauce

INGREDIENTS

- Eggplant - 2 pcs.
- Olive oil - 4 tbsp.
- Garlic - 2 cloves
- Paprika - ½ tsp.
- Sea salt
- Black pepper, freshly ground
- Tomatoes (canned, cut into pieces) - 400 g

PREPARATION

1. Preheat a barbecue or cast iron grill pan with ribbed bottom. Cut the eggplants into 1 cm circles and place in a colander. Sprinkle with salt, press down with a plate and let sit for 15 minutes. Rinse and pat dry with a paper towel.
2. Preheat 1 tbsp. l. butter in a skillet over low heat. Add the sliced garlic and paprika. Cook for a few seconds, salt and pepper. Stir in the tomato pulp, bring to a boil over high heat, reduce heat and simmer for 15 minutes.
3. Brush the eggplant with the remaining oil and grill on a barbecue or skillet for 3 minutes on each side, until golden brown. Pour over cooked tomato sauce and serve.
4. Enjoy your meal!

26 Grilled Vegetables with Herbs

INGREDIENTS

- Young zucchini - 2 pcs, Young eggplants - 2 pcs, Bulb onions - 2 pcs.
- Bulgarian pepper - 3 pcs, Tomatoes - 4 pcs, Chili peppers - 4 pcs.

For the marinade:

- Olive oil - 3-4 tbsp. spoons, Hops-suneli - 2 tsp
- Dried thyme - 2 tsp, Freshly ground black pepper - to taste
- Salt to taste

PREPARATION

1. Cut the eggplants into circles. I prefer to cut them thicker - about one and a half to two centimeters. Cut the zucchini in the same way.
2. Peel the onions. And cut into circles. With him, too, "small" is not necessary. Put onions on skewers so that the rings do not fall apart when grilling.
3. So that the skewers are not too long and do not interfere with cooking, I cut them with a pruner.
4. Remove the core from the bell pepper, and then cut it into 4 pieces.
5. Tomatoes don't need any special preparation; they just need to be washed. Do the same with red chili peppers.
6. Let's move on to preparing a mixture for pickling vegetables. In a deep bowl, mix the suneli hops, thyme, salt and freshly

ground pepper. Pour the spices with olive oil. Mix the contents of the bowl.

7. Transfer vegetables to a deep bowl. Fill them with a mixture of oil and aromatic herbs. Distribute the mixture evenly over the entire surface of the vegetables (except for tomatoes and chili peppers - we will not marinate them, because we did not cut the skin in any way, and the marinade simply will not penetrate inside). Leave the vegetables to marinate for 15 minutes.

8. Grilling coals. While preparing the grill, another 10-15 minutes passed, which means that the vegetables were completely marinated. Not immediately, already in a slight heat, without fear that they will burn, spread the vegetables on the grill. After about 4-5 minutes, turn the vegetables over and grill for the same amount of time.

27 Grilled Potatoes and Tomatoes

INGREDIENTS

- Young potatoes - 900 g ☐ White wine vinegar - 1 tsp ☐ Olive oil - 7 tbsp.
- Chives inflorescences (chopped) - 45 g (3 tbsp. L.)
- Cream tomatoes, yellow - 4-5 pcs.
- Salt and black pepper to taste

PREPARATION

1. Switch on the grill to preheat to medium temperature. Boil the potatoes in lightly

salted water until soft, for about 10 minutes.

2. Meanwhile, prepare the tomato and potato dressing. In a small bowl, combine chives, wine vinegar and 5 tablespoons of olive oil. Throw boiled potatoes in a colander, let the water drain, and then cut each tuber lengthwise, in half. Add salt and pepper to taste.
3. When the grill is hot enough, take the potatoes one half at a time, dip the slices in the remaining oil and place them on the wire shelf, cut side down. Fry for about 5 minutes.
4. Turn potato halves over and fry for about 3 minutes. Place the fried potatoes in a large bowl, drizzle with the dressing and stir.
5. Place the tomato halves on the wire rack and fry for 3 minutes.

6. Serve potatoes with tomatoes.

28 Sweet Potato Salad

INGREDIENTS

For the salad:

- Small sweet potato - 1 kg
- Pea leaves mung bean - 140 g
- Soft cheese (crumbled) - 1 glass
- Dried caramelized cranberries - 1/2 cup
- Vegetable oil
- Chili pepper (seeded and finely chopped) - 1 pc.
- Pumpkin seeds (roasted, peeled) - 1/2 cup

For refueling:

- Red wine vinegar - 1/4 cup ☐ Fresh cilantro (chopped) - 2 tbsp.
- Salad onion (chopped) - 2 tbsp.
- Fresh ginger (chopped on a grater) - 1 tbsp.
- Liquid honey - 2 tbsp.
- Orange peel - 2 tsp ☐ Dijon mustard - 2 tsp ☐ Salt - 1/2 tsp.
- Vegetable oil - 1/2 cup

PREPARATION

1. Prepare the dressing. In a small bowl combine vinegar, cilantro, onion, ginger, honey, orange zest, mustard and salt, mix well, then add oil and mix well again. Set aside.
2. Prepare salad. Grease the grill grate with vegetable oil, and turn on the grill for

preheating to medium-high temperature (180-200 degrees).

3. Peel the sweet potato and cut into slices about 1.2 centimeters thick. Boil sweet potatoes in water until soft and cartilage, for about 5-6 minutes. Dry and brush with vegetable oil.
4. Place the sweet potatoes on the grill, cover the grill and fry the sweet potatoes on both sides (only 8-10 minutes) until tender. Toss the fried sweet potatoes in a large bowl with the chili and the dressing.
5. Put green mung bean leaves on a serving dish, sprinkle with cheese and cranberries. Put potatoes on mung bean and sprinkle pumpkin seeds on the sweet potato salad.
6. Serve the sweet potato salad immediately.

CHAPTER FOUR
Poultry Recipes

29 Chicken Breast Grill with Soya Sauce

INGREDIENTS

- 750 g chicken breast fillet For Sauce:

- 2 tablespoons soy sauce
- 1 tablespoon honey
- 2 cloves of crushed garlic
- 1 teaspoon of grated fresh ginger
- 1 teaspoon of brown sugar
- 1 tea glass of olive oil

- Salt
- Black pepper

PREPARATION

1. Take the ingredients for the sauce in a deep bowl and mix.
2. Chop the chicken breast into large pieces. Take the chicken meat into the bowl containing the sauce and mix. Stretch the film and let it rest in the refrigerator for 1 hour. Index of meats in bottles, cook on the grill. Serve hot.

30 Chicken Recipe with Sauce

For 4 people

Cooking time: 20 minutes

INGREDIENTS

- 800 grams of fillet chicken breast
- 2 tablespoons olive oil, 1 tomato
- 1 clove of garlic, 1 small onion bulb
- 1 teaspoon tomato paste
- 1 teaspoon hot sauce (or 1/2 teaspoon powdered red pepper)
- 1 teaspoon of oregano, 1 teaspoon of coriander (if desired)
- 1/4 teaspoon cumin

PREPARATION

1. If you have time to extend the marination period of chicken meat in the sauce mixture you prepare, leave for 1 hour in the refrigerator.
2. You can also cook the chicken with sauce on the grill or pan on greasy paper.
3. Cut the breasts of fillet chicken which you wash in water and dry with paper towel into long thin strips.
4. For the sauce mixture; after peeling the skin, drain the juice of the onion you planed. You can use the posa portion for another meal.
5. Grate the tomato with the thin portion of the grater. Put the onion juice and grated tomatoes in a deep mixing bowl. Mix with olive oil, grated garlic, tomato paste, hot sauce, thyme, cumin and coriander.

6. Take the chopped fillet chicken breasts into the mixing bowl and cover them and leave them in the refrigerator.
7. For long periods of rest (at least one hour and one night if you have time), pass the chicken meat horizontally to the wooden skewers.
8. Cook as soon as possible by inverting the duplex on a pre-heated pan or grill.
9. According to desire; Share with your loved ones on heated lavash with the addition of curly lettuce leaves, ring-cut red onions and tomato slices.
10.

31 Savory Chicken Thighs with Grill Marinade

Cooking time: 30 to 60 min

INGREDIENTS

- One toe garlic (crushed)
- 1/2 tablespoon mustard
- 2 tsp sugar (brown)
- One teaspoon chili powder
- Pepper (black, freshly ground)
- 1 tbsp olive oil
- 5 pcs chicken lower leg

PREPARATION

1. For the spicy chicken legs with grill marinade, mix the garlic with the mustard, the brown sugar, the chili powder, a pinch of salt and freshly ground pepper. Mix with the oil.
2. Rub in the chicken thighs with the marinade and marinate for 20 minutes.
3. Put the chicken thighs in the basket and push the basket into the Pressure cooker. Set the timer to 10-12 minutes.

4. Fry the chicken thighs at 200 º C until brown. Minimize the temperature to 150 º C and fry the chicken thighs for another 10 minutes until they are cooked.
5. The spicy chicken leg with barbecue marinade with corn salad and baguette serve.

32 Organic Grilled Italian Chicken Recipe

INGREDIENTS

- 1 pound of organic chicken breast without bones
- 1/4 cup Italian dressing / marinade

PREPARATION:

1. Burn your grill over medium heat.
2. If using a grill pan, set the burners to medium heat.
3. Marinate chicken in Italian dressing for at least 1 hour.
4. Spread the chicken breast with Italian dressing / marinade and place on the grill.
5. Boil your chicken and stick it with your Italian dressing / marinade throughout the cooking time.
6. Cook until your chicken reaches the internal temperature of about 20 minutes and turn the chicken halfway to the other side.

33 California Grilled Chicken

INGREDIENTS

- 3/4 c. balsamic vinegar
- 1 teaspoon. Garlic Powder
- 2 tbsp. honey
- 2 tbsp. extra virgin olive oil
- 2 tsps. Italian spice
- Kosher salt
- Freshly ground black pepper
- 4 boneless chicken breast without skin
- 4 slices of mozzarella
- 4 slices of avocado
- 4 tomato slices
- 2 tbsp. Freshly cut basil for garnish

- Balsamic glaze for drizzling

PREPARATION

1. In a small bowl whisk balsamic vinegar, garlic powder, honey, oil and Italian spices and season with salt and the pepper. Pour the chicken and marinate for 20 minutes.
2. When you are ready to grill, heat the grill to medium high. Grate the oil grills and chicken until charred and cooked through, 8 minutes each side.
3. Top chicken with the mozzarella, avocado and tomato and lid grill melt, 2 minutes.
4. Garnish with basil and then drizzle with some balsamic glaze.

34 Grilled Chicken

INGREDIENTS

- 1 whole chicken, dry
- 3 tbsp Paleo melted cooking fat
- 3 tbsp fresh rosemary, finely chopped
- 2 onions, peeled and quartered
- 4 carrots, peeled and cut into slices
- 2 peppers, chopped
- 2 lemons cut in half
- Sea salt and freshly ground black pepper

PREPARATION

1. Preheat the oven to 204 C.
2. Place the chicken, face down, on a cutting board. Cut along both sides of

the spine from one end to the other with kitchen scissors and remove the spine. Turn the chicken breast over and open it like a book. Firmly press the breasts with the palm to flatten them.

3. In a small bowl, mix cooking fat and 2 tablespoons of fat. of rosemary.
4. Rub the chicken with 2/3 of the fat and rosemary mixture and season the chicken to make it taste with sea salt and ground pepper.
5. Cover a large baking sheet with aluminum foil.
6. Place the chicken right on the baking tray and then surround it with the vegetables and lemons.
7. Pour the mixture of fat and rosemary remaining on the vegetables and season to taste.
8. Put the baking sheet in the oven for 1 hour or until a meat thermometer

indicates 73 C into the thickest part of the breast.

9. Remove the chicken from the oven; squeeze a little lemon juice and go.

35 Wings Recipe with Sauce

For 4 people   Preparation Time: 20 minutes
Cooking Time: 50 minutes

INGREDIENTS

- 1 kilogram chicken wing
- 4 tablespoons sunflower oil
- 4 tablespoons of milk
- 2 tablespoons yogurt
- 1 teaspoon tomato paste
- 1 teaspoon hot sauce
- 2 cloves of garlic
- 1/2 teaspoon of grape vinegar
- 1/2 teaspoon of honey, 1 bay leaf
- 1 teaspoon of oregano
- 1 teaspoon fresh ground black pepper
- 1 teaspoon of salt
- 1 sprig of fresh rosemary

Tip of the Winged Sauce Recipe: Extending the marinating mixture will increase the flavor of chicken wings.

PREPARATION

1. Wash the chicken wings in plenty of water and remove excess water with the help of paper towels.
2. Grate the garlic. Mix sunflower oil, milk, yogurt, tomato paste, hot sauce and honey in a large bowl.
3. Add grated garlic, bay leaf, thyme, freshly ground colored black pepper, extracted rosemary branches and salt. Mix all the ingredients.
4. Put the chicken wings in the sauce mixture you prepared and place them in a single row on the oven tray.
5. Bake in a pre-heated 180 degree oven for 45-50 minutes. Serve hot wings, which draws the sauce and flavored with spices.

36 Chicken with BBQ Sauce

INGREDIENTS

- 4 Pieces of Chicken Legs

- Salt, Pepper
- 300 ml. BBQ Sauce or Ketchup
- 500 gr. Celery Stalk
- 1 Tablespoon Liquid Oil ☐ Sugar
- 1 Dessert Spoon Vinegar

PREPARATION

1. Thoroughly wash and clean the chicken thighs, then salt and pepper.
2. Place the thighs on the baking tray with the skins facing down.
3. Bake in an oven heated to 200 ° for 15 minutes, turn over and cook for another 15 minutes.
4. Spread a thick layer of barbecue sauce or ketchup on them and cook for another 5 minutes.
5. Cut the stems of celery finely, chop the leaves.

6. Celery stalks in oil for 5 minutes, sprinkle with a pinch of sugar sprinkle, circulate vinegar.
7. Add the minced leaves, salt and pepper.
8. Serve the chicken with vegetables and sauce.

37 Grilled Chicken with Ranch Sauce

INGREDIENTS

- Chicken
- 1 lb. chicken (4 lb.)
- 10 ml (2 teaspoons) salt
- 5 ml (1 teaspoon) of garlic powder
- ½ lemons

- 1 recipe of ranch vinaigrette, Salad
- 4 celery stalks, minced
- 1 bulb of fennel, finely chopped
- 1 green onion, chopped
- 30 ml (2 tablespoons) chopped fennel leaves

- 30 ml (2 tablespoons) of olive oil
- 15 ml (1 tablespoon) lemon juice

PREPARATION

1. On a work surface, using the chef's knife or kitchen scissors, remove the bone from the back of the chicken. Flip the chicken and cut in half in the center of the breasts. Place the pieces in a large glass dish. Sprinkle chicken skin with salt and garlic powder. Rub the outside and then inside of the chicken with the cut part of the lemon. Thoroughly coat with 1/2 cup (125 mL) ranch vinaigrette. Cover and refrigerate 12 hours.

2. Preheat half of the barbecue at high power. Oil the grill on the off side.
3. Drain the meat. Place the chicken on the off-the-grill section, skin side on the grill. Close the barbecue lid. Bake 45 minutes while maintaining a temperature of 200 ° C (400 ° F). Return the chicken and continue cooking for 35 minutes or until a thermometer inserted in the thigh, without touching the bone, indicates 180 ° F (82 ° C) maintaining a temperature of 200 ° C (400 ° F). Finish cooking on the lit section of the barbecue to mark the chicken.

CHAPTER FIVE
Lamb Recipes

38 Lamb Shashlik with Honey Sauce

INGREDIENTS

- Boneless lamb shoulder (cut into 5 cm cubes) - 400 g
- Garlic (minced) - 1 clove
- Ground cumin (cumin) - 1 tsp.
- Dried red pepper, flakes - 1/4 tsp.
- Wine red vinegar - 2 tsp ☐ Honcy - 1 tsp.
- Pitted green olives (chopped) - 2 tbsp.
- Fresh mint (chopped leaves) - 2 tbsp.

- Extra virgin olive oil - 3 tbsp.
- Salt to taste
- Couscous for garnish (optional)

PREPARATION

1. In a medium bowl, mix the chopped meat with 1 tablespoon oil, 1/2 teaspoon garlic, 1/2 teaspoon cumin, 1/2 teaspoon salt, and red pepper flakes.
2. Turn on the grill to preheat to a high temperature.
3. In a small bowl, combine the vinegar, mint, honey, olives, leftover garlic, cumin and olive oil.
4. String the meat on 4 small skewers and place on the grill rack. Fry for about 3-4 minutes on each side.
5. Put the kebabs on a plate (optional - with a side dish), pour over with honey sauce.

39 Grilled Lamb

INGREDIENTS

- Lamb steak on the bone, 2.5 cm thick - 8 pcs. (120 g each)
- Ground cinnamon - 0.75 tsp
- Ground black pepper - 0.5 tsp.
- Ground allspice - 0.25 tsp ☐ Ground cumin (cumin) - 0.25 tsp.
- Salt - 1/8 tsp.
- Ground red pepper - 1/8 tsp.
- Vegetable oil
- Lime wedges for serving

PREPARATION

1. Turn on the grill to preheat to mediumhigh temperature. Grease the wire rack with oil.
2. In a small bowl, combine cinnamon, black pepper, allspice, cumin, salt and red pepper. Rub the lamb steaks with this mixture on all sides.
3. Place the steaks on the grill rack and cook for 4-5 minutes on each side.
4. Serve the lamb steak with lime wedges. Garnish to taste.

40 Grilled Leg of Lamb

INGREDIENTS

- Lamb leg - 2 kg
- A mixture of 5 peppers - 2 tbsp.
- Smoked salt (coarse salt with fried crispy bacon) - 1.5 tbsp.
- Cumin - 1 tsp
- Anchovies - 20 g
- Rosemary - 8 sprigs ☐ Thyme - 8 branches
- Garlic - 5 cloves

PREPARATION

1. Let's prepare a mixture for rubbing. To do this, heat a mixture of five peppers

over maximum heat in a dry frying pan until they smell.

2. Next, grind the heated mixture of peppers in a mortar with smoked salt and 1 teaspoon of cumin. Rub the leg with this mixture from all sides. Next, we make several punctures 5 cm deep.
3. We sprinkle the leg with anchovies, garlic (cutting the cloves in half, dipping them into the rubbing mixture), rosemary, thyme.
4. Rewind with a rope and bake in a charcoal grill, in an indirect way, that is, placing coals around the leg. I baked for about two hours at a temperature of 200220 degrees. Next, wrap the leg in foil and leave for 15 minutes. Served with grilled bell peppers and pesto. And also with mushrooms marinated in mayonnaise, soy sauce, garlic oil, coriander. Enjoy your meal!

41 Lamb (Lamb) Marinated In Anchovy Sauce

INGREDIENTS

- Young mutton (lamb), tenderloin - 1 pc. (650-700 g)
- Bulb onions - 1 pc.
- Salted anchovies, in oil - 1 can (150 g)
- Capers - 2 tbsp
- Olive oil - 3 tbsp.

PREPARATION

1. Make cuts on the meat crosswise, about 1 cm deep. Peel the onion and cut into 4 pieces. Drain the anchovies and capers. Combine the onions, anchovies, capers and olive oil in a blender until a paste.

Brush the cooked lamb sauce so that the mixture goes into the cuts. Leave to marinate in the refrigerator for 30 minutes.

2. Preheat the barbecue or grill (there should be no flame on the coals). Roast the tenderloin at low heat for 40 minutes, turning frequently. Place on a plate and leave in a warm place for 10 minutes.

3. Cut the meat into 1cm slices. Serve with unleavened bread and herbs. You can serve chickpea sauce (hummus) with fried lamb.

4. Enjoy your meal!

42 Grilled Leg of Lamb

INGREDIENTS

- Boneless leg of lamb (lamb meat) - 1.3 kg
- Vegetable oil (sunflower)
- Coarse salt
- Ground black pepper

Marinade:

- Olive oil (extra-virgin) - 2 cups
- Fresh herbs (oregano, thyme, savory, parsley, rosemary), coarsely chopped - 2 cups
- Garlic, coarsely chopped - 24 cloves
- Zest of 4 lemons, finely grated
- Coarse salt - 3 tsp

- Ground black pepper - 2 tsp.

PREPARATION

1. Cut the leg of lamb in the middle, leaving 1 inch (2.5 cm), and open like a book. Beat to a thickness of about 3 cm over the entire surface. Mix all marinade ingredients. Leave ½ cup. Place the rest of the marinade and meat in a plastic bag and close it. Stir the contents of the bag. Leave the meat to marinate in the refrigerator for at least 8 hours (up to 1 day). Turn the bag of meat periodically.

2. Remove the lamb from the marinade and pat dry. Leave at room temperature for 1 hour.

3. Preheat the grill to 175-190 degrees (when you can hold your hand without discomfort over the wire rack at a distance of 10 cm for 4-5 seconds). Lightly oil the wire rack. Season the meat with salt and pepper on both sides.

Fry, pressing the tongs against the wire rack

for 5-6 minutes (after 3 minutes, turn the meat 90 degrees). Turn the lamb over, brush with reserve marinade. Fry the other side for 5-6 minutes, also turning the meat 90 degrees.

4. Leave the meat for 5 minutes and then chop. Serve with the remaining marinade. Enjoy your meal!

Lamb Chops in Lemon-Garlic Marinade

INGREDIENTS

- Olive oil - 1 tbsp.
- Fresh lemon juice - 2 tbsp
- Lemon zest, grated on a fine grater - ½ tsp.
- Oregano - 2 tbsp l. fresh grass or 2 tsp. dried
- Chopped garlic - 6 cloves (2 tbsp. L.) ☐ Salt - ½ tsp.
- Ground black pepper - ¼ tsp.
- Young lamb loin with ribs (cut off all fat from the meat) - 8 pcs. 110-120 g each

PREPARATION

1. Preheat broiler or grill to medium heat.

2. Prepare the marinade for the ribs. In a small bowl, combine the oil, lemon juice, zest, oregano, garlic, salt and pepper.
3. Place the ribs in a resealable plastic bag and pour in the marinade. Close and mix the contents of the bag. Leave at room temperature for 20 minutes (up to 1 hour).
4. Remove the pieces of meat from the marinade. Roast lamb ribs on the grill or under the broiler to the desired degree of doneness (if 4-5 minutes on each side - the meat will be fried on the outside and pink on the inside). Enjoy your meal!

44 Grilled Lamb

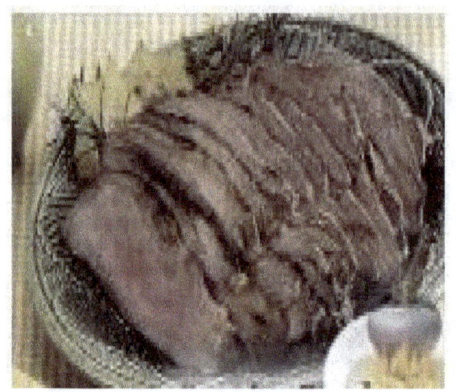

INGREDIENTS

- Dijon mustard - 1 glass
- Soy sauce - 1/2 cup ☐ Olive oil - 2 tbsp.
- Fresh rosemary (chopped) - 1 tbsp.
- Ground ginger - 1 tsp
- Garlic (minced) - 1 clove
- Boneless lamb shank - 1 pc. (2-2.5 kg)

PREPARATION

1. In a bowl, combine the mustard, soy sauce, olive oil, rosemary, ginger and garlic. Take 2/3 cup of this mass and refrigerate.

2. Pour the rest of the marinade into a large plastic bag with fasteners. Clean the meat from fat and films, if any. Place the lamb in the marinade bag, shake well, close the bag and refrigerate overnight.
3. Switch on the grill to preheat to medium temperature. Remove the meat from the marinade and place on the oiled grill rack. Place the lid on the grill and cook the meat for about 50-70 minutes (the meat thermometer should show a temperature of 75 to 85 degrees). Transfer the finished meat to a cutting board, cover with foil and let rest for 10 minutes, then cut the meat into slices and serve immediately with the reserved marinade.

45 Lamb Cutlet Burgers

INGREDIENTS

- Pita thin small - 8 pcs. (30 g each)
- Minced mutton - 450 g
- Feta cheese (crumbled) - 0.25 cups
- Ground cumin - 0.25 tsp
- Ground black pepper - 0.25 tsp.
- Vegetable oil
- Red onion (rings) for serving (optional)
- Alfalfa sprouts for serving (optional), Cucumber (slices) for serving (optional) For the sauce:
- Frozen green peas (thawed) - 2 cups
- Garlic - 2 cloves

- Fresh mint, leaves - 0.5 cups ☐ Olive oil - 1.5 tsp.
- Water - 1 tsp, Salt - 0.25 tsp

PREPARATION

1. Place all the ingredients for the sauce in the bowl of a kitchen processor and grind until smooth. Set the sauce aside. Turn on the grill to preheat to medium-high temperature.
2. In a large bowl, combine the minced meat, cheese, cumin and black pepper. Divide the minced meat into 4 parts, form a round cutlet from each.
3. Grease the grill rack with vegetable oil, place the cutlets on it and fry for about 6 minutes on each side. Transfer the cutlets to a plate and rest for 5 minutes.
4. Cut each cutlet in half lengthwise. And cut each pita cake in half lengthwise, but not until the end. In the middle of each pit, apply 1 tbsp. spoonful of sauce, put

on one cutlet and a choice of onions / sprouts / cucumber.

5. Serve burgers right away.

46 Lamb with Mint and Bell Pepper

INGREDIENTS

- Lamb shoulder - 4 pieces (200-250 g each, 2.5 cm thick)
- Dried rosemary - 1 tbsp
- Coarse salt
- Ground black pepper ☐ Fresh lemon juice - 3 tbsp ☐ Olive oil - 1 tbsp.
- Dijon mustard - 2 tsp
- Red sweet pepper, finely chopped - 1/3 cup
- Fresh mint, finely chopped - ½ cup ☐ Green onions, chopped - 1 pc.

PREPARATION

1. Preheat the grill (broiler). Rub the meat (2.5 cm thick pieces) on both sides with rosemary (¾ tsp), salt (¾ tsp), pepper (¼ tsp). Cook until desired, about 4 minutes on each side (or slightly longer until the meat is medium), turning the pieces once.

2. Combine lemon juice, olive oil and mustard. Add bell peppers, mint and green onions. Serve the roast lamb warm with the prepared sauce over the meat.
3. Pour a cup water into a large skillet (to cover the bottom), add ¼ tsp. salt. Bring to a boil. Add 3 medium zucchini, cut into circles. Cook for 3-4 minutes. Discard in a colander, transfer to a bowl. Drizzle 1 tbsp of zucchini. l. olive oil. Sprinkle with 2 tbsp. l. chopped green onions, salt, pepper and stir.

47 Lamb with Yoghurt Sauce

INGREDIENTS

- Natural fat-free yogurt - 1/2 cup ☐ Chopped mint - 1 tbsp.
- Lemon juice - 1 tsp ☐ Garlic (minced) - 1 clove ☐ Salt - 1/2 tsp.
- Ground black pepper - 1/2 tsp.
- Lamb (tenderloin) - 4 pieces (250 g)
- Vegetable oil for lubrication

PREPARATION

1. Preheat the grill.
2. Mix the first 4 ingredients. Add 1/8 tsp. salt and 1/8 tsp. pepper. Refrigerate.
3. Season the meat with salt and pepper. Grease a frying pan with oil, put the lamb on it, fry for 3-4 minutes on each side.

   Serve with yoghurt sauce.

48 Lamb Cutlets with Eggplant

INGREDIENTS

- Lamb mince - 500 g
- Garlic (peeled and finely chopped) - 2 cloves

- Cilantro leaves (finely chopped) - 1/2 cup
- Goat cheese (original Halloumi) (shredded) - 100 g
- Salt and black pepper to taste
- Small eggplants (cut into halves) - 16 pcs.
- Olive oil
- Natural yogurt - 140 g (1/2 cup)
- Turkish bread (sliced and fried)
- Lettuce, finely chopped chili and mint leaves for serving

PREPARATION

1. In a large bowl add minced lamb, cilantro, half garlic, cheese, salt and black pepper to taste, mix well. Form 4 cutlets from the resulting mass and set aside.
2. Preheat the grill to medium heat; grease the eggplants and place on the wire rack, fry for about 3 minutes on each side. Transfer to a plate, set aside.

3. Sprinkle the lamb cutlets with butter and place on a wire rack, fry for about 4 minutes on each side.
4. In a small bowl, place the yoghurt and the remaining garlic and mix well.
5. Put yogurt sauce on the slices of bread, put lettuce leaves on top, and on them put lamb cutlets, fried eggplant and chili. Decorate with mint leaves.

49 Grilled Lamb with Rhubarb Sauce

INGREDIENTS

For grilling:

- Lamb steaks on the bone, 2.5 cm thick - 12 pcs. (120 g each)

- Garlic (cut into thin slices) - 2 cloves ☐ Olive oil - 1 tsp.
- Black peppercorns (crumbled) - 1 tsp.
- Vegetable oil for grilling grill For the sauce:
- Rhubarb (finely chopped) - 6 stems ☐ Onions (finely chopped) - 1 pc.
- Liquid honey - 1/3 cup
- Apple cider vinegar - 1/4 cup
- Golden raisins - 1/2 cup
- Chili pepper (seeded and finely chopped) - 1 pc.
- Garlic (finely chopped) - 4 cloves
- Whole boxes of cardamom (tied in a gauze bag) - 8 pcs.
- Fresh cilantro (chopped) -1 glass

PREPARATION

1. Prepare the lamb sauce. In a medium saucepan, combine rhubarb, onion, honey, vinegar, raisins, chili peppers,

garlic and a bag of cardamom. Pour 1/2 cups water over the contents of a saucepan, put on medium-high heat and bring to a boil. Reduce heat to low, cover saucepan and cook lamb sauce until rhubarb is very soft, about 15 minutes. The finished sauce should be tasted and, if necessary, add a little more honey or hot pepper. Remove the saucepan from the stove, remove the bag of cardamom and add the cilantro to the saucepan. This lamb sauce can be served warm or chilled.

2. Rinse the lamb steaks, dry with a paper towel and stuff with garlic plates (with a sharp knife you need to make holes in the meat for bacon). Grease the meat on all sides with olive oil and roll in crumbled black pepper. Leave the meat to rest at room temperature for 30-60 minutes.

3. Grease the grill grate with vegetable oil and turn on the grill to preheat to medium-high temperature. Place the meat on the grill rack and grill the lamb for about 3-4 minutes on each side (the temperature on the meat thermometer should reach 70 degrees). Once the grilled lamb is done, serve the grilled meat with the sauce.

50 Grilled Lamb with Parsley and Rosemary

INGREDIENTS

- Young lamb meat (sirloin) - 2 kg
- Olive oil - ½ cup, Garlic - 3 cloves
- Parsley - 4 tbsp

- Fresh rosemary - 3 sprigs
- Dried chili pepper (flakes) – pinch
- Salt pepper
- Parsley (for garnish), Extra virgin olive oil

For the salad:

- Cream tomatoes - 4 pcs.
- Cherry tomatoes (on a branch) - 500 g
- Yellow tomatoes (desirable) - 250 g
- Fresh basil - 1 bunch, Garlic - 1 clove
- Small red onion - 1 pc, Olive oil of the first cold pressing - 3 tbsp.

PREPARATION

1. Cut off excess fat from the meat and cut the fillet in half. In a large bowl, stir together the olive oil, finely chopped garlic, chopped parsley, rosemary leaves, and chili flakes. Season with salt and black pepper to taste. Place the lamb in the cooked marinade and rub the meat

well with the mixture. Leave in the refrigerator for at least 1 hour.

2. Preheat your barbecue or charcoal grill. Roast the lamb until the desired degree of doneness is desired (8-10 minutes on each side - the meat stays pink inside). Transfer to a plate, cover with foil and leave in a warm place for 20 minutes.

3. Cut the tomatoes lengthwise into 4 pieces (leave the cherry tomatoes intact, with stalks), crush a clove of garlic and cut the onion thinly into rings. Stir all the ingredients of the salad, season with salt and pepper and stir gently.

4. Slice the meat diagonally and place on a platter. Sprinkle with parsley leaves and drizzle with olive oil. Serve with vegetable salad.

5. Enjoy your meal!

CONCLUSION

Each time you barbecue, you must make an important decision about the type of smoke wood to use. Beef, pork, poultry, and seafood all have different flavours depending on the wood. It's also true that certain woods are associated with and complement specific types of meat.

Many of the top barbecuing experts keep quiet when it comes to revealing their exact secrets because grilling or smoking with BBQ wood is such an important part of their repertoire. Everything from the type of wood they use to their own sauce recipes to how they season the meat before grilling can become top secret weapons in their quest to stay on top of the barbecuing world.

www.ingramcontent.com/pod-product-compliance
Lightning Source LLC
Chambersburg PA
CBHW070916080526
44589CB00013B/1326